Music
of the
Heart

Poems of Love, Pain, and Hope

L.R. Phoenix

authorHOUSE®

AuthorHouse™
1663 Liberty Drive
Bloomington, IN 47403
www.authorhouse.com
Phone: 1-800-839-8640

Published by AuthorHouse   01/25/2013

ISBN: 978-1-4817-0903-3 (sc)
ISBN: 978-1-4817-0902-6 (e)

Library of Congress Control Number: 2013901072

Contents

CHAPTER 1

Love

Here I Stand

I stand here before you naked and open
Bless me please with a wonderful token
A token of your word to be my clothing
On your word I stand and am floating.

I repent my Lord of the sins I bare
I am filled with hope and void of despair
The pages are turning in my book of life
I look forward to more prosperous times.

Bless my hands, bless my feet.
Bless my entire family
My future wife, my darling girl
She's a sparkling gift worth more than diamonds or pearls.

Watch us Lord and protect us always
No matter if we are in bright or dark days.
Keep us whole and reliant on you.
Let us recognize all that you do.

Whether it's big or small let our praises be to you
It is you who helps us and makes our dreams come true.
Let us live in the light and not in the dark
Let your love capture us deep within our heart.

To My Family

To my family whom I love so much
Words cannot explain just how precious
Such joy you have brought into my life
You're the two apples of my eye

My son, so loveable, so sweet and cute
Brings me such warmth when I'm around you
Babs, my love, the song of my heart
Complete is how I feel, I pray we never part

I entered your lives in such an untraditional way
Cuts & bruises were gathered along the way
I'm happy in the role that I play
It will be even greater as the past fades away

You both are what I work for
I'm so glad to do so
A greater life for us is in store
For you two I'd work my fingers to the bone

I thank you for the love you've shared with me
If I haven't been before I'll be more reciprocating
But I hope you both know that I love you
And that I would do anything for you

Our Love

So crazy we're here today,
Never thought I could love this way.
Happy times are here for us,
Happiness in God we trust.

We've had hard times,
No doubt about that.
With no will to give up,
We fought back.

So pure is what I feel for you,
Our love is strong and it will endure.
And soon a chapter will close forever.
We'll be on our knees thanking God together.

Value

You have blessed me so richly,
And taught me more about me,
The value in truth,
The value in honesty

Through the love of my life
I've learned many things,
The value of patience
And the blessings it brings.

How to be a team player
Teaching me love's layers
Helping me to change a bit of who I am
So I can contribute to a love that will forever stand.

So Blessed

You make my heart go out of control,
So much that it speaks a language it doesn't know.
The power of our love is like a raging tide,
Sprung from a well deep inside.

Your love whispers softly like the wind
It flows from a source with no beginning or end.
When we love we dance like fire.
Flames like these can never expire.

Your love is my love and mine is yours.
Ours is a golden love with so many blessings in store.
Brought together by God, it must be destiny,
For us to live happily

You overwhelm me and are a far cry above the rest
You are the lifeline in my beating chest
When I am with you I am at home and my souls at rest
You have enriched my life and I am truly blessed

Power of Love

Love me tender, love me sweet,
Love me as the oceans deep.
In your heart let love swell,
In your heart let me dwell.

A delightful kiss brings joy abound,
Love's energy flows all around,
To tease and tug at our heart strings,
To stir up the blessings that love can bring.

A little me, a little you,
Results of what love can do.
Here we are, here as one,
Slaves to this thing called love.

Crystal Lake

Staring at this beautiful Crystal Lake,
The sun gently kisses my face.
Thinking of one who is so dear to me,
Massaging my lungs as I take her into me.

Enriching my blood and giving me truth,
I yearn for her love like a child and their sweet tooth.
She caresses my soul and leaves me with no control,
Lord let her be mine to have and to hold.

The softness of her lips and smell of her perfume
She fills me to capacity and overflows because there is no room
Looking down the shore I see lilies in bloom
Bringing memories of our love and how it grew

This Crystal Lake is such a beautiful place
A cool breeze surfs across my face
I am powerless against her gentle embrace
My soul retires so that I may never leave this place

Honey

Your love is so sweet it sticks to me
Flowing in and out of my bloodstream
Even though we are apart
You still produce the honey in my heart

I feel you in my veins and I feel you in my gut
I only had a moment to love you and it wasn't enough
Like a beehive that's hanging from a tree
You're my honey bee and you live inside of me

Many thoughts of you are so very lovely
At times I have the physical taste of your honey
Even though we're apart you're still the twinkle of my eye
Happy thoughts keep me sunny and my days bright

I miss you love, you are my heartbeat
I feel your presence flowing in and out of me
I know you're gone but it's still you I see
I'll never forget my sweet tasting honey

Summer Moon

Moonlight shines on a summer's night
I'm wishing I had my baby by my side
The moons glow dances on the ripples of the water
It's beautifully mesmerizing and my mind wanders

I think on a love that has passed
A love that I surely thought would last
But it does live on in my heart
Eternally singing its love song

Fading in and out of reality, I see you dance across the sky
The stars are your playthings in the warm summer night
My soul leaps at the sight of you
How can I forget how much I love you?

You come to me and I'm wrapped in your embrace
Soothing warmth rests across my face
The sun greets me as I squint at high noon
I long for night fall and my summer moon

CHAPTER 2

Pain

A Heart's Pain

Everyday my heart lays broken and torn
I struggle vehemently but I can't pull out the sword
It's as though my heart is a cosmic joke
It lays barely beating and bleeding its death note

Alone in an icy tundra even the cold can't cool my pain
I feel like a soldier who has been beaten and slain
I waiver from tree to tree in my forest of pain
So dark are my days and always drenched in rain

Tortured by memories of recent times
I knew happiness once upon a time
Love used to be a friend of mine
Now I wander this wasteland broken and dying

Yet in the distance I see a glimmer of light
A twinkle of hope and an end to the pain and strife
So I walk on, gravely wounded, believing I'll be healed
I will not die until I find a love that is real

A Moment In Time

A moment in time is what we had
Now it's gone to never-never land
Maybe never to be seen again
What we had was from deep within

A moment in time was when I loved you
A moment in time is what we knew
We loved so deeply and purely
But the moment has gone and set us free

A storm came through and pierced our bubble
It lay in our hearts for future troubles
Contaminated by the impurity of what was
It slowly chewed away at our love

Until there was nothing but contention
Our bubble stretched from all the tension
Still in love but not in the moment
Desperately trying to find atonement

For our wrongs against each other
Wrongs against our love
We hoped to go further
But yet instead we tumbled.

A moment in time is what we had
I'm still in love and my moment stands
A moment in time falls to our past
Now alone we stand

Barren Heart

I thirst for you like the desert thirsts for rain.
My pain is so unbearable that my cheeks bare teardrop stains. What remains are cacti full of memories. I cut one open so that it may quench me.

A dry barren wasteland is what my heart is today. Tattered and frayed from the agony that has come its way. Wondering when its barren ground will heal? When it will feel love once again?

When will it feel the blessed showers of a caring soul? So that the hearts field of dreams may grow.
Hiding the scars of a painful past,
While new flowers bloom on a love that will last.

A Fool

I cannot breathe, I cannot breathe
Why is the air denied to me?
My heart pierced like it was speared
Forced to let go of what I held so dear

What happens when you have no home?
What happens when you're broken, desolate, and alone?
When the future you saw is now gone
Like Bill Withers "ain't no sunshine" because she is gone

The world goes about its way
Yet I smile and put on the happy face
While inside I swim in an acid pool
I am tormented by the way love had me fooled.

The Lonely Road

Walking down this lonely road
Barefoot, wet and oh so cold
Maneuvering around broken pavement with every step
I noticed the trees weeping as I wept

Its fall again but it was summer yesterday
Not much longer until winter comes this way
Over there beyond the horizon
I see frostbitten trees and plants dying

My fingertips tingle as the cold breeze takes hold
My nose runs as chills grab hold of my soul
My movements become slow as life refrigerates my bones
I fall prisoner to this long lonely road

Not dead but also not alive
I feel crystals fall from my eyes.
A living statue that's lost to time
My light fades as the world passes me by.

When Love's Not Enough

Some say love is all you need
But what happens when it's not enough
What happens when you fight for something worthwhile?
Only to be kicked to the dust.

When love fails, where do you go?
Do you have the answer because I need to know?
A truer love I have never found
But now bare hands have ripped my heart out

My lungs burn and I cannot breathe
A devouring flame incinerates me
How do you move through the devastation?
When love leaves you without hesitation

Shackled by loss and whipped by grief
A suffocated soul since the light was removed from me
I lay weeping and yearning for her touch
What do you do when love is not enough?

Come Back To Me

Since you left things haven't been the same
The rain is always seen, even on sunny days
This wounded heart barely beats
It is broken, bleeding, and weak

Moving forward is such a struggle
My heart has been silenced and muzzled
Faint is the beating of my heart
I've lost sight of life and my world is dark

Come back to me oh summer breeze
Love me hard and love me deeply
Renew the greatness we once shared
Fill my lungs with much needed air

Hold me forever and don't let go
Let us be bound to each other to have and to hold
Love me tender and love me sweet
Love me as the ocean is deep.

Remember our love and let me in
I may look fine but I'm bleeding within
Heal this damaged heart and give me air to breathe
Remember our love and come back to me.

My Greatest Pain

My greatest pain is when she walked away
Cut out my heart and threw it away
This lonely road is my only friend
There's a storm in my eyes, my soul breaks and my knees bend

As each day goes by I can't help but wonder why
Why did love fail? Why did hers die?
This lonely road full of cracks and glass
Barefooted I walk in a pain that forever lasts

Red tears stain my cheeks
My body riddled and crippled with grief
Bloodshot eyes because I have found no sleep
Death's hand rests on my shoulder preparing to take me.

Is there a healing? Lord please let me know!
Will I ever have a love to nurture and grow?
Will I have someone that will never leave?
Even though times get rough will stand by me?

I'm sure mercy will come my way one day.
The bright warm sun shining the storm clouds away
Healing my wounds although scars may remain
Taking me away from this road of pain

Until then I wait as this pain continues to saturate
My every pore and my every being continues to deteriorate
Until that day I find relief at last.
Until that day that love returns and forever lasts.

Drifting The Canal

Fighting the current I thrash and gasp for air
The force of the water threatens to pull me further into despair
Barely any strength left, water begins to fill my lungs
Filling them with the eerie smell of death and all its muck

To the bottom I go, the surface is fading fast
I'm holding to life but that doesn't last
Consciousness falls away like sand from my hand
My life has been taken and I am in a dark land

Creatures of pain torture me
Heart pain, soul pain, and spirit pain voraciously attack me
If I weren't already dead I surely would be now
This everlasting orgy of pain keeps me down

I fight and fight trying to regain my life
I feel an empowerment as I regain sight and see light
I swim to the top but the pains hold tight and don't stop
I find my counsel of three, my raft, to give me strength to stay on top

And so it is here that I drift
On my raft floating under a bridge
Waiting for a rescue I try to paddle
Waiting for my heroine as I drift the canal

CHAPTER 3

Hope

Breathe

As I exhale my pain flows out
Bit by bit removing the stormy clouds
Inhaling hope and faith for the future
A reuniting of a love rekindled in the near future.

A future of love and understanding
With God first in all of our future plans
Our love brings a diamond ring
A princess cut and the sun makes it bling.

A couple of kids to add to the mix
An older brother to play Legos with
So happy in love our family is
I raise my hands high and give praise to Him!

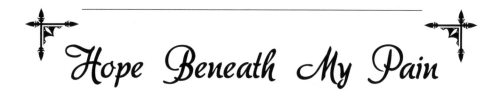

Hope Beneath My Pain

My breath is shallow because I am dying
Always crying on the inside and sighing
It takes so much strength to take a normal breath
My heart skips beats under such painful stress

This is a test that I sometimes wonder if I'll survive
Inside I am dead though it appears I'm alive
This pain, this knotting wicked pain won't go away
It won't leave me be, it just sits and stays

I just want to wake up from this nightmare
I can barely stay afloat in my despair
This pain is like endless needles pricking my heart
Everyday my soul is torn apart

My love, my darling love, how I miss you so
How I wish we didn't part. I am so alone
I miss your touch and I miss your smile
I still believe our parting is only for a while

So we take this time to learn and grow
When we come back together our love will be better shown
And awaiting you will be a diamond ring
And we will be united as king and queen.

Out Of The Darkness

My heart explodes with the force of a supernova
My life as I know it is now over
Taken is the joy of my being
My whole nervous system is failing

I loved her so much and I still do
Imprisoned in this void, what am I to do?
I stare at the darkness and it stares back at me
Greedily tonguing the life out of me

The light in me fades as my essence joins the void
My eyes are the last to begin to join the void
Then from the darkness a light cuts the darkness in half
I reappear fully and am shown my path

I don't know where the path leads
I'm hoping it leads back to her
My Lord please guide me
So that my destiny blooms like a flower

On this road I see healing in the distance
On the way I pick up the heart that I thought was missing
Bringing to memory my visions and dreams
And at the end of this path I see her and me.

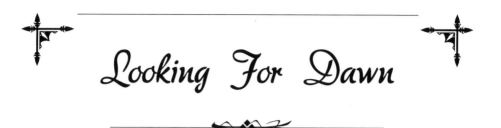

Looking For Dawn

The season has changed and I'm a dead flower
There's no life in me, I have no power
My heart is gone. She up and left me
Laying on my raft in this water drifting

My nights are cold and my days are bitter
I still have dreams and fantasies of being with her
But I'm all alone waiting by the phone
Hoping to hear her say baby come home

Hallucinations of her touch
Brings visions and feelings of love
I see her reach for me as I look up
But am brought low by a ghost's touch

Vapor is all that is before me
My vision of late is so hazy
Life as I knew it is long gone
Yet in the night I still look for the dawn

My Soul Awaits

Walking through life with sadness in my eyes
My soul grows weary and is soon to die
In and out my memories fade
I can only see life with eyes of haze

The damage I took, and yet I still live
My heart falls out as I try to hold it in
Darkness has made a companion out of me
I am blind but hopeful that one day I'll see

I wait to feel the warmth of the sun
A pretty face who knows I'm the one
Someone who treats me how she wants to be treated
Someone who lets me know that I'm needed

I await this thing, they call it love
Let it be filled with mercy and blessings from above
Our lives illuminated in glory and majesty
Ruled by our Lord, ruled by our King

Eagles Wings

My tears flow like a waterfall
And as the waterfalls so goes my happiness
Undressed, revealing my nakedness and my loneliness
I have no clothes for my body to caress

I obsess for what I once had
Yet in the distance I hear laughs. I see the clouds pass
Dark, showing me its nature
A creature unrelenting, unrepentant, showing me no favor.

Raining its hatred upon my person hoping to worsen
What I feel and seal away my hopes and dreams
Yet these are not easily sealed and removed
My hopes and dreams cannot be entombed

It cannot be taken because I have a destiny
I am of power, I am strength, I am a king
Made wonderfully by the Most High King
I rise above the storm and fly high above its sting.

On eagle's wings I fly with the warm sun on my back
I am battle weary but the Son has got my back
And I clamp and hold tight to my destiny
I stand strong believing in all that was promised to me

Beyond Hope

So hard these past few weeks have been
So much anger and pain that no one wins
We lost each other and our hearts are breaking
For it to mend will be quite the undertaking

Our love was strong and I knew my search was done
We believed it was a blessing from above
We envisioned ourselves walking down the aisle
And at the end watching rice touch the sky

I still hope beyond hope that we will get there one day
Walking hand in hand as the music plays
Appreciating each other for who we are
Loving each other whether near or far

You're my babe and mean the world to me
We broke up but you're still a huge part of me
So I hope beyond hope that we'll be together again.
We will be stronger than ever and our love will never end.

My Prophecy

A year from now we will be back together
Ready to start over and facing life together
Before this happens it will be our time to heal
From how this all started, we shall learn how to deal

In this time I would have made some money
Being blessed by the Lord with milk and honey
Returned to my place in God's eyes
Living fruitfully in His light

In this time you will have gone through changes of your own
Being spiritually fed and spiritually grown
Finding your land of milk and honey
No more stressing about money

When the time comes we'll start as friends first
Hanging out and laughing, unaffected by past hurts
Then we will fall in love again and make love you see
Starting over again but not like the beginning.

Until then we go on to heal
Always remembering the love we feel
Always knowing no one can replace us
Knowing our love is right and just

I feel this in my heart
I feel this in my soul
For a short while we will be apart
Then we will be one to have and to hold.